At Home with God

A Child's Book of Prayer

Volume I

Text and Photography by

Marlene Halpin, Ph.D., Dominican

SCRIPTURE TRANSLATION
Psalm translations from the Hebrew,
with theological interpretation made
with children in mind, by JoAnn
Stanley, Dominican

Cover photo by Philip Coblentz

Send all inquiries to:
Tabor Publishing
200 East Bethany Drive
Allen, Texas 75002–3804

Printed in the United States of America

ISBN 0–7829–0361–4

1 2 3 4 5   97 96 95 94 93

Contents

Introduction

Welcome to a happy book!

God is happy.
God wants you to be happy.
God helps you to be happy.

How does this work?
Oh, in lots of ways!
Here's one:

Find a place at home where you like to be.
Find a place at home where your body fits.
You and God can meet there.
When you and God meet,
you can let God know:
- what you did today,
- what happened to you today,
- how you feel about what happened.

God loves to hear from you.
God always loves you.
You can count on it!

How do you get started?
Maybe this book will give you some ideas.
But when you get your own ideas, *use them first!*

Mystery

You know how you feel
"way down deep inside."

How do you find your
"way down deep inside"?
(Sh! It's a *mystery!*)

You know when you love someone.

Can you put love into a box?
Can you tie it with a ribbon?
(Love is a *mystery!*)

You know God made you.

Can you *smell* God?
(God is a *mystery!*)

A *mystery* is when:
• we know it's true,
• we don't know how,
• we don't know why.
But we know it's so.

When you love God from
"way down deep inside,"

when God loves you from
"way down deep inside,"

it's a wonderful mystery

that we call *prayer.*

That's why praying is awesome!

Questions Children Ask about Prayer
How can God listen to everyone at the same time?

There's the sun.

What does the sun do?

IT SHINES!

What does the sun shine on?

EVERYTHING! EVERYONE!

There's the rain.

What does the rain do?

IT GETS THINGS WET!

What does the rain rain on?

EVERYTHING! EVERYONE!

SUN shines on everyone and everything. That's the way the sun is.

RAIN rains on everyone and everything. That's the way rain is.

There's God.

What does God do?

GOD listens to everyone at the same time. That's the way God is.

GOD loves everyone at the same time. That's the way God is.

Isn't God wonderful?
Isn't God awesome?

Maybe you want to take a minute and tell God how you feel about this.

Why do we fold our hands when we pray?

Try it!
Put your hands together
with your palms touching.

Now, can you throw a ball?　NO!
Can you eat pizza?　NO!
Can you put things away?　NO!

Why?

Because when your hands
are folded like this,
it means:

This is God's time!

You are with God.
God is with you.
It is special time.
When your hands are
folded like this,
it is holy time.

While your hands are still
folded, love God and let
God love you for a little while.

Birthdays

Dear God,

*I LOVE birthdays! I love a
birthday best when it's mine!*

Here's why I love birthdays, God.

Let God know why
you love birthdays.

You can *tell* God, of course.
Maybe you want to *show* God
pictures in your mind of a
Happy Birthday. (Do you want
to sing "Happy Birthday to You"
so God can hear the music?)

*In my family here's how
we celebrate birthdays.*

Show God (like a TV in your
head), or tell God, how your
family acts on birthdays.

*Here's what we do in our school
when someone has a birthday.*

What's your school like on
birthdays? Let God know.

*Do you know what I like
about birthdays? Or what I
wish were different?*

God loves to know from you,
so tell God what you like.
Tell God if there's something
you wish were different.

*If you didn't make me, God,
I wouldn't have a birthday!*

*Thank you for making me.
I love you, too.*

You and God spend a little
time together, so the two of
you can enjoy loving each other.

We ask God:
Who are we that you should be mindful of us,
that you should so much care for us?

Psalm 8:5

God's House

Dear God,

I know you are everywhere.
That's the way you are.

I know you are in
special places, like in
my heart, and in church.

We go to church, sometimes,
God.

Do you know how I feel about
going to church?

God, it's fun to meet you
in different places!

Thank you, God, for being
everywhere!
Thank you, God, for loving me!

Tell God how wonderful
that is!

Let your heart love God
extra for a minute.

Tell God when you go
to church.

Let God know what it's
like for you to go to church.
(God likes it when you
are honest!)

Think about meeting God:
- in your heart,
- in your home,
- in your church.

Maybe you can tell God when
you will visit again in church.

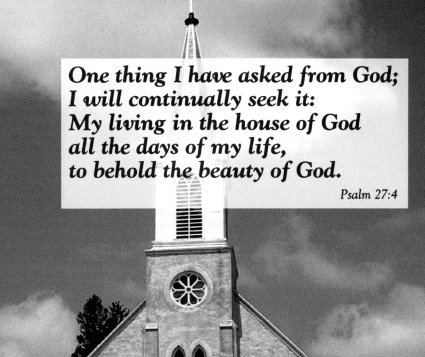

One thing I have asked from God;
I will continually seek it:
My living in the house of God
all the days of my life,
to behold the beauty of God.

Psalm 27:4

Going to Bed

Dear God,

Sometimes I'm glad when it's bedtime. Sometimes I want to stay up longer.

Since I got up this morning, God, this is what happened.

During the day, God, I met some people. Here are the people I met today.

When I think about my day, God, do you know what I wish?

Well, God, please bless all the people I met today. Help each one of us to be good to each other and to love you.

God, please give us a peaceful night. Let us wake up happy.
Good night, God.

Let God know how you feel about going to bed tonight.

Tell God the things you did today and how you feel about them.

Name the people you met. Tell God about each one, and what you did. Show God your heart and how you feel about each person.

What do you wish? Would you do something a different way? Ask for help, if you want to.

Put everyone you love in your heart. You and God look at them together, and together love them.

With fullness of life
I will lie down and sleep;
for you alone, O God,
shelter me in safety.

Psalm 4:9

I'm Sorry

Dear God,

I'm sorry.
I wish I could go back
and do it over again.

Tell God what you are
sorry for.

If you could do it over
again, what would you do?

God, sometimes I get
all mixed up. I don't
mean to do bad things.

Tell God why it is so
hard to be good all of
the time.

Listen to God in your
heart. Maybe God will
give you a new idea.

God, I'm glad you really
know me. I'm happy you
love me. I'm happy you
always give me another
chance.

Ask God to help you.

Then you and God spend
a few minutes just
loving each other.

Thank you, God.
Bye-bye.

O God, help me to know your ways.
Help me walk in your truth,
   for you are the God
   who is with me always.

Psalm 25:4–5

Missing Someone

Dear God,

I feel like I have a big hole inside of me.

Someone I love isn't here anymore. I'm lonesome.

Tell God who you are lonesome for.

Maybe your brother or sister went away to school, or got married.

Maybe your parents got divorced.

Maybe your friend moved.

Whom do you miss?

God, I miss _____ . (Tell God the person's name.) Look at my heart, God.

Show God your heart. Is it sad? Is it crying? Is it hiding? Let God have a good look. Let God know how much your heart really hurts.

God, please take care of _____ . (Tell God the person's name again.)

Put the person into your heart. You and God look at that person. You and God together love her or him.

Please bless us both, God.

Thank you.

God watches over your coming and going,
from now until forever.

Psalm 121:8

Scared

Dear God,

Sometimes I get scared.
I mean the kind of scared
that makes me feel bad inside.

Tell God things that scare
you. Let God know what or
who is bothering you right now.

God, this is hard to explain.
Maybe you'd know better if
I show you where it hurts.

Let God see your heart, or
your tummy, or your neck, or
what part of your body feels
scared. Let God see how you
look when you are feeling bad.

Please, God,
   hold me,
   love me,
   help me remember
you are always with me
(even if I don't feel like you are).

Let's stay together a little
bit more before I have to go.

You and God stay together a
little while. (Maybe you
want to imagine sitting on
God's lap.)

O God, when I begin to get afraid,
I will trust you.

Psalm 56:4

A Special Person

Dear God,

Today I want to tell you
about a special person I know.

Tell God the name of someone
who is really special for you.

Let me tell you, God, why
_____ (say the person's name)
is so special.

Tell God in words or pictures
or feelings, or just KNOW
about it together. God's very
good at that.

Well, God, what do YOU
think about my Special Person?

Listen with your heart in case
God wants you to understand
some more now.

Or, just be quiet with God
while you think about and love
your Special Person.

When you are ready, you might
say to God:

Dear God,

Please bless my Special Person,
(say the person's name),
extra today. And please bless
me, too. Help me to remember
you are with me all day.

I have to go now. Bye.

I delight in your holy people.
My greatest pleasure is to be with them.

Psalm 16:3

Thank You!

Dear God,

Everything comes from you.
I want to say "Thank you!"

Tell God some *people* you are
thankful for, and some
things, too.

See how many things you can
name. (Maybe you want to
draw some of them.)

God, I want you to know
how very, very glad I am
that you give me these people
to love, and things to have.

You might invite God to
look at your heart and see all
the gladness and thanks you
have there. Take your time.

Please help me, God, to love my
family and friends. Show me
how to take care of things and
to share them. I guess that's
a good way to say "Thank you."

You and God look together at
the people you know, and the
things you have. Give God
praise by being *glad* for
everyone and everything you have.

Maybe you can spend a little
time just being glad.

Thank you for loving me,
God. I love you, too.

O God, you alone do wondrous things.
Your care is everlasting!
Give thanks to the God of heaven,
for God's care is everlasting!

Psalm 136:4, 26

What Is God Really, Really Like?

Dear God,

Suppose, today, I just think
about you.

I know you made EVERYTHING.
I know you made EVERYONE.

Think about that by yourself
for a minute or so.

I know you love everyone in
the whole world. You love us
just the way we are. So, God,
what are YOU really, really like,
to be able to do that?

Welcome God into your mind.
Welcome God into your heart.
When you are so close
together, think about God.

While your brain thinks,
and while your heart loves,
let God see how you are getting
to know who God really is.

Then you might want to say:

God, I praise you for being God!
God, I love you for being God!

God, I adore you!

Just be *glad* that you are
beginning to know God
as God really, really is.

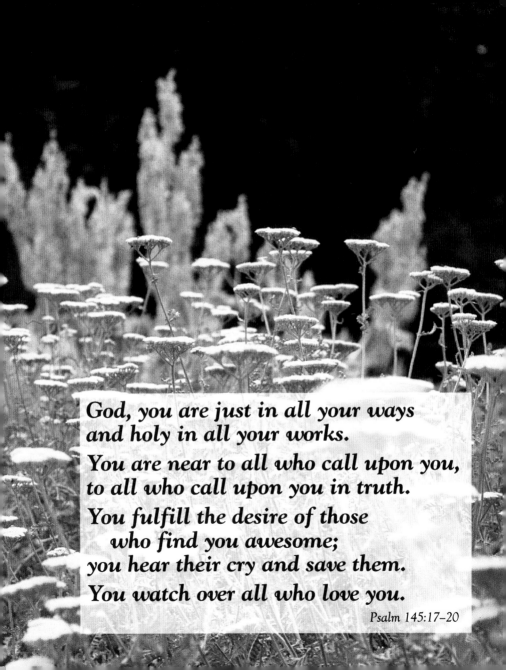

God, you are just in all your ways
and holy in all your works.

You are near to all who call upon you,
to all who call upon you in truth.

You fulfill the desire of those
who find you awesome;
you hear their cry and save them.

You watch over all who love you.

Psalm 145:17–20

Why, God?

Dear God,

*I cried today because my
pet died. God, you know my pet.*

Remind God about your pet:
a dog, or cat, or gerbil, or
fish, or whatever yours was.

My pet's name is _____ .

Tell God the name. Describe
your pet to God: what it looks
and sounds and feels like.

God, I really love _____ .

Tell God some stories about
your pet, stories that show
why you love your pet.

I know that my pet loved me, too.

Tell God how you know this.

*I cried when I had to
say good-bye to _____ .*

Let God know how you said
good-bye.

*God, I don't like it when
animals or people I love die.
Why does it happen?*

Listen with your mind and
heart. Some things are very
hard to understand. It takes
a long time. Even then we
don't feel good. Be with God,
missing your pet.

*God, I miss _____ .
Please take care of _____ .
For a little while, God, will
you hold me in your love?*

You are safe in God's love.

O God, hear my voice as I cry out!
Have feeling for me! Answer me!
My heart tells me to seek God's face.
God, I look for your face.
Do not hide your face from me.

Psalm 27:7–9

Some More Ideas

We can pray about *anybody*.
We can pray about *anything*.
We can pray about *whatever happens*.

It would take very, very long to make a list.
But we don't have to make a list.
What is a good thing to do is this:

Every day invite God into your mind and your heart.
Give God a tour so God can see what you think,
and how you feel. Then you can tell, or ask, whatever
you want. Or sing a little. Or just be quiet a bit.

You can pray in the special place you like, or you can
do it *anywhere* and *anytime*.

God *never* is too busy to pay attention to you.

You *can't* make a mistake. However you meet God,
God loves it. And God loves you.

The only mistake you can make is to forget God.

But you love each other too much to forget, don't you?
(Well, at least most days! And God understands.)

Isn't God truly *awesome!*